Author:
Rupert Matthews was born in Surrey,
England, in 1961. He was educated at his local
school and has made a lifelong study of history.
He has written over 150 books since becoming
a full-time writer.

Artist:
David Antram was born in Brighton, England,
in 1958. He studied at Eastbourne College of Art
and then worked in advertising for fifteen years
before becoming a full-time artist. He has
illustrated many children's nonfiction books.

Series Creator:
David Salariya was born in Dundee,
Scotland. He has illustrated a wide range of books
and has created and designed many new series for
publishers both in the UK and overseas. In 1989
he established The Salariya Book Company. He
lives in Brighton, England, with his wife,
illustrator Shirley Willis, and their son Jonathan.

Editor:
Stephen Haynes

Editorial Assistant:
Mark Williams

Published in Great Britain in 2007 by
The Salariya Book Company Ltd
25 Marlborough Place, Brighton BN1 1UB

ISBN-13: 978-0-531-18746-3 (lib. bdg.)   978-0-531-13925-7 (pbk.)
ISBN-10: 0-531-18746-2 (lib. bdg.)   0-531-13925-5 (pbk.)

All rights reserved.
Published in 2008 in the United States
by Franklin Watts
An imprint of Scholastic Inc.
Published simultaneously in Canada.

A CIP catalog record for this book is available
from the Library of Congress.

Printed and bound in China.
Printed on paper from sustainable sources.

You Wouldn't Want to Be a Mayan Soothsayer!

Written by
Rupert Matthews

Illustrated by
David Antram

Created and designed by
David Salariya

Fortunes You'd Rather Not Tell

Franklin Watts®
An Imprint of Scholastic Inc.
NEW YORK • TORONTO • LONDON • AUCKLAND • SYDNEY
MEXICO CITY • NEW DELHI • HONG KONG
DANBURY, CONNECTICUT

Contents

Introduction

You are the son of a Mayan soothsayer or holy man, living near the city of Copán in about AD 710. There are many different Mayan states covering a large part of Central America. Copán —in the country which will later be called Honduras—is one of the most powerful. It is ruled by King Waxaklahun Ubah K'awiil, whose name means "Eighteen are the faces of the god Kawiil." King Waxaklahun is beginning a major project to rebuild the city of Copán.

An old friend of your father's runs a school that trains boys to be soothsayers, priests, and other holy men. If you learn to be a holy man, you can go to the city of Copán itself and try to become an important man. Mayan holy men have many difficult duties to perform. You will have to spend long hours learning to read and write and to recognize the hundreds of Mayan gods.

You would rather be a farmer in your peaceful village in the rain forest. You don't want to go, but you have no choice.

The Soothsayer's Son

As the son of a Mayan soothsayer you are going to spend your entire life in the world of religion. In Mayan society nearly everybody works in the same sort of job as their parents. You start school at the age of about seven. The school is run by an elderly priest whose job is to teach you and other sons of holy men the basic skills. The first thing you will learn is how to count, and how to do sums in writing. Arithmetic is vital to Mayan religion.

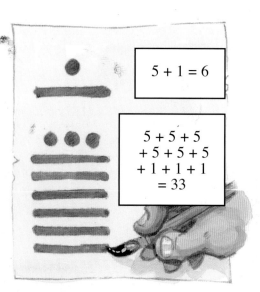

$5 + 1 = 6$

$5 + 5 + 5$
$+ 5 + 5 + 5$
$+ 1 + 1 + 1$
$= 33$

MAYAN NUMBERS. The Maya have two ways of writing numbers. The simple method (left) is to use a ball for the number 1 and a horizontal line for the number 5. Just keep drawing lines and balls until you have the correct number.

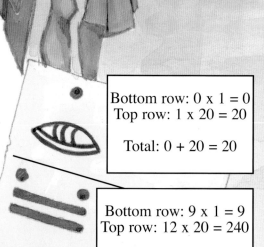

Bottom row: $0 \times 1 = 0$
Top row: $1 \times 20 = 20$

Total: $0 + 20 = 20$

Bottom row: $9 \times 1 = 9$
Top row: $12 \times 20 = 240$

Total: $9 + 240 = 249$

COMPLEX SUMS. For larger numbers you need to use a more complex system (right). The bottom row is in units of one, the second row up units of 20, the third line up units of 400, and so forth. An oval shape means zero. So a single ball above a zero means 20 (no units + one lot of 20). Try it!

Handy Hint

Avoid getting chosen to look after the garden. You will be expected to empty the toilet pots over the plants as fertilizer.

YOUR CITY. Copán is one of the larger Mayan cities. There are about 100 cities, scattered across the Yucatán Peninsula (in modern Mexico and Belize) and nearby areas. Some are independent; others are ruled by larger cities.

NORTH AMERICA

CENTRAL AMERICA

SOUTH AMERICA

The Mayan world

Chichén Itzá

Cobá

Jaina

Uxmal

GULF OF MEXICO

YUCATÁN PENINSULA

CARIBBEAN SEA

Palenque

Tikal

Quiriguá

Copán

PACIFIC OCEAN

Choosing a Path

At the age of about 14 you take your final exams at the basic school in Copán. If you pass, you will attend a graduation ceremony where you will be presented with your own writing desk. You will also be chosen to be a trainee by one of the many holy men of Copán. But if you fail your exams, you will be thrown out of the school. Then you will have to be a workman in the fields, and that is very hard work indeed.

What Are Your Options?

SHAMAN. The shamans live in rural villages, where they do magical spells for farmers. They are poor men who carry around skulls, herbs, and frogs for their spells. Not a very desirable job.

Handy Hint

Have a bath, borrow some expensive jade jewelry, and brush your hair before graduation. You want to look your best so you are chosen for a good job.

BOOKKEEPER. All the temples of Copán need men who can write and add up reliably, to keep records of their wealth and estates. Steady work, but dull— you can do better than this.

CHRONICLER. Rich noblemen employ chroniclers to record their family history and tell exciting stories at parties. This could be a fun job—but only if you enjoy showing off.

SOOTHSAYER. Definitely the best job available. As a sacred priest you will be an important and respected person. Yes, this is the job for you!

The Calendar of the Gods

GLYPHS. Each word in Mayan has its own glyph—a picture-like symbol. You will have to learn hundreds of these.

PUNISHMENT. Your master can punish you however he likes. He may make you breathe the smoke from burning chili peppers.

LUNCHTIME. Your master will have tasty meals, but you will be lucky to get cornbread and tomato sauce.

The Maya use a sacred calendar called the Tzolk'in Haab, which is based on three cycles. The first has 13 days, numbered 1 to 13. The second cycle has 20 days, each with a different name such as Ahaw, Imix, or Chuwen. The third cycle is made up of 18 months of 20 days each, plus 5 special days at the end of the year, making 365 in all (sound familiar?). The cycles mesh together in such a way that each day for 52 years has a different name. You will need to learn all this by heart—sorry.

THE TUN. Once you have learned the Tzolk'in Haab, you will be taught the long-count calendar, the Tun. This lasts 5,126 years, so it's a good thing you don't have to learn it by heart.

Don't worry, son. It's easy when you know how.

HOLY DAYS. Use the Tzolk'in Haab to decide which days are sacred to which gods, which days are lucky or unlucky, and when various festivals take place.

So Many Gods!

Just another 130 to go...

The Maya have more than 150 different gods. You will need to learn all their names, their powers, and the rituals that they like. Then you can advise people how to win the favor of the gods and so succeed in life. The one who looks like a young man with silky hair is Hun, the maize god. He not only controls the growth of maize—a basic food for the Maya—but also helped create the world from a shapeless flood by fighting the evil Lords of Xibalba.

EK CHUWAH. He's the god of profit. If you know which days are sacred to him, you can advise merchants of the best times to do business deals.

CHAAK. Farmers revere this god, who looks after rain and irrigation. By studying Chaak you can tell when to plant seeds, water crops and harvest them.

Handy Hint

Learn as much as you can about Kawiil, god of power. He is the patron god of the king of Copán, and you want to keep in with the king, don't you?

BABIES. You will be asked to advise parents on their children's future. Try dangling a spindle over a baby to see if the child will be any good at spinning.

OOPS! If you make a mistake you're in trouble. Your master will cut your finger to drip a blood sacrifice onto the god you insulted.

Royal Sculptures

I f you do well as a soothsayer, a nobleman might take you into his house as his personal priest. So when the king himself asks you to dedicate a new stele— a stone pillar carved into the image of a god—in the main square of Copán, you must do your very best. Hire a band of musicians and dancers to perform the sacred dances, and make sure everyone is wearing the right clothes before you begin the ceremony. Sacrifice grains of maize to Hun, the maize god. King Waxaklahun is dressed as Hun for the day.

Well, it all goes well and King Waxaklahun himself gives you a job. What will he expect you to do?

DANCE MASTER. The king will need to perform sacred dances during rituals. It's your job to teach him—but if he makes a mistake, be careful how you tell him!

HOLY BREWS. You will have to learn the recipes for the many different soups, stews, and brews that need to be drunk to honor the various gods.

Handy Hint

Learn how to sew. You may need to repair costumes before a ceremony to avoid being punished if things go wrong.

Gulp!

ROYAL SACRIFICE. Women from the royal family offer their blood to the gods by having their tongues stabbed with needles—that's another one of your jobs.

ANIMAL SACRIFICE. Use a knife of sharp obsidian stone to kill rabbits, then look at their intestines to see whether the gods are happy or not. You're not squeamish, are you?

15

The Wayeb Festival

The last five days of each year are known as Wayeb, and the Wayeb Festival is the most important ceremonial event of the year.

As the king's priest, you need to light a fire to Itzamna, the moon god. You then have to carry a small statue of the death god in a procession to a shrine outside the city, where King Waxaklahun sacrifices a turkey.

This isn't my favorite part.

BAD OMENS. It's up to you to shake off any bad omens that occur during Wayeb. Build a great fire of timber, wait for it to get white-hot, then walk across it barefoot.

HUN STATUE. The statue of the god Hun by the city gates is repainted during Wayeb.

FORTUNE-TELLING. At the end of Wayeb you will forecast the king's future using a stylized map of the world. Uh-oh: this year it's bad news.

16

TURKEY SACRIFICE.
The king chops the head off the turkey, then throws the body toward the city to ensure a prosperous new year.

The Ball Game

Ball games are held to honor the gods, but are also great social events. As the king's soothsayer you must consult the Tzolk'in Haab calendar to decide which god the games are for, and what rituals will be needed. You must then attend the game to watch out for any cheating. King Waxaklahun has built a new ball court out of stone. It's about 66 feet long, with a flat central ground and sloping sides. The players use their arms and legs to knock a small rubber ball up the sides of the court, trying to hit one of six stone targets. Points are scored for hitting the target, but lost for allowing the ball to hit the floor. It's a rough game, so the players wear heavily padded outfits.

BETTING. The Maya love to bet bags of maize on the outcome of the sacred ball game. As a soothsayer and priest you might have inside information—use it well!

CROWD TROUBLE. Huge crowds gather to watch ball games. Those at the back might not see much.

FRIENDLY MATCH. Games sacred to lesser gods, such as the merchant god Ek Chuwah, are happy affairs to celebrate the god and his works.

DEADLY SERIOUS. In games sacred to major gods such as Kawiil, the losers are sacrificed to the god.

Warrior Cults

SPEARS. Every Mayan warrior has a spear made of wood and tipped with obsidian.

WAR CLUBS. Many Mayan warriors like to use war clubs made from heavy pieces of timber edged with sharp obsidian.

The city of Quiriguá, which is ruled by Copán, rebels. King Waxaklahun orders the warriors of Copán to march to war. As the royal soothsayer you must march with him. Before leaving, you need to attend to the various warrior cults and societies of Copán.

ANIMAL HATS (below). Warriors wear hats made from stuffed animals to show to which warrior cult they belong.

IRON RATIONS (below right). Campaign food is not very appetizing: dried corn, dried fish, and peanuts.

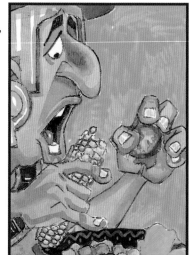

Handy Hint

Volunteer to carry the statue of the death god on your back. You will then be sacred, and nobody will try to kill you.

Grrrr

JAGUAR SACRIFICE. Before setting off to war, the king asks you to sacrifice a savage jaguar. He believes this will give him the courage and ferocity of the big cat. Your only weapon is a stone knife. Good luck!

The Battle of Quiriguá

The army of Copán marches to Quiriguá, confident that they will defeat the smaller army of the rebel city. But as they approach Quiriguá they are ambushed by an enemy force led by the nobleman Kahk Tiliw Chan Yopaat, whose name means "Fiery Lightning Sky God." The men of Copán are taken by surprise, and many run away. As Waxaklahun's soothsayer you must stay by the king's side, even though he is wounded and captured by the men of Quiriguá. Because you are carrying the statue of a god, your life is spared.

WHISTLING. Before a battle the warriors whistle loudly to show how brave and strong they are.

TRUMPETS. Conch shells are blown like trumpets to give orders across the battlefield.

TAKE COVER.
The first action is always a hail of javelins and slingshot, so all the warriors take cover behind their shields.

Handy Hint

Prisoners are often sacrificed to the gods, but skilled men are spared to work for their captors. Make sure they know you are a skilled soothsayer.

CHARGE! Having thrown their javelins, the warriors charge.

Death to Copán!

A New King

After the battle, Waxaklahun is sacrificed to the gods by Kahk Tiliw Chan Yopaat, now King of Quiriguá. You return to Copán to be met by the new ruler, King Kahk Joplaj. He makes you Ahkuhan, or Reader of the Holy Books. You are now Chief Priest for all of Copán. You are given a fine house and many servants.

CHOCOLATE. For the first time in your life you will be allowed to drink hot chocolate, the holy food. You can have as much as you like.

HOLY LAKE. Every year you must offer jade to the gods at the underground lake of Naj Tunich.

EASY LIFE. You now have servants to carry you everywhere on a litter.

Handy Hint

Nobody may disturb the Ahkuhan when he is reading the sacred books. Take the chance to have a quiet doze in the library.

I hope he's nicer than the last one.

BLOODY WORK. One of your new duties is to sacrifice humans to the gods. Keep your knife sharp so you're ready for action at any time.

Planet-Gazing

One of your most important jobs as Ahkuhan is to watch the movements of the stars and planets. These will tell you the best times for planting, harvesting, and other vital activities. Go to the roof of a temple on a clear night, and use a system of crossed sticks to measure the angles and directions of the various objects in the skies. Watch the Moon, Venus, and Mars very closely, and record the positions of their rising and setting every day as accurately as possible. You will be adding your records to those of earlier priests dating back over 500 years. By comparing past events to the movements of the planets, you can predict what is likely to happen in the future.

BAD OMENS. The Maya believe that comets are warnings of important changes affecting the city or its king.

TIME FOR WORK. The Maya plant their maize on the day that the Pleiades vanish. You must advise farmers which day this is.

VENUS. The planet Venus follows an eight-year cycle in the sky. Venus is the planet linked to war, so use the cycle to advise the king when to fight.

SEVEN MACAWS. The position of this constellation (we call it the Big Dipper or the Great Bear) indicates the start of the hurricane season.

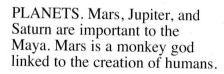

PLANETS. Mars, Jupiter, and Saturn are important to the Maya. Mars is a monkey god linked to the creation of humans.

Handy
Hint

Point out the movements of the stars to the king. If you forget to tell him something important you may be in trouble.

A Life of Ease

After you have been Ahkuhan for some years, it is time to retire. You are given a good farm within sight of the temples where you used to work. Your house looks onto a courtyard with a barn and other buildings. Outside are gardens filled with vegetables, and fields of maize. You no longer need to wear your large, heavy ceremonial clothes, stay up late at night watching stars, or even do much farming, now that you are rich enough to have servants. You can relax and spend all your time with your family and friends.

WHEELS. Although they don't use carts or wagons (as far as we know), the Maya do use wheels —for children's toys.

FISHING. Paddling in a canoe to catch fish is a popular Mayan hobby. Now that you are retired, you will finally have time to enjoy yourself.

VENISON. You are still an important man, so locals will try to please you by handing over special treats and presents, such as deer to eat.

Handy Hint

Keep a close eye on your stores of food. Your foreman might be tempted to steal some to sell.

GET MARRIED. Now that you are rich and famous, all the girls want to marry you. Make your choice, then marry her in a ceremony that involves tying your cloaks together.

SOOTHSAYER'S SON. When your eldest son is about seven years old, send him off to your old school. Tell him everything will be fine.

Glossary

Ahkuhan The chief priest and chief librarian of a Mayan city, responsible for the sacred books.

Chaak The Mayan god of rain. He is usually shown as an old man.

Chronicler A type of historian who each year writes down the important events that have happened in a chronicle—a book rather like a diary, but organized year by year instead of day by day.

Conch shell The shell of a large marine mollusk. The shells could be made into trumpets by cutting off one end and blowing hard.

Copán One of the largest of the Mayan cities. It was founded by King Yax Kukmo in about AD 426 and collapsed into civil war around 822. The ruins have been excavated and are now open to the public.

Ek Chuwah The Mayan god of profit. He is usually shown as a man with a long nose.

Glyph A symbol used in writing systems where each symbol represents a complete word, unlike our alphabet, where each letter represents a single sound.

Hun The Mayan god of maize. He is usually shown as a young man.

Itzamna The Mayan Moon god, who was sometimes thought to have created the Earth. He is usually represented as an old man with a hooked nose.

Jade A hard, green stone used in jewelry. The Maya valued jade more highly than any other jewel or metal, even gold.

Javelin A small, light spear that could be thrown at enemies.

Kawiil The Mayan god of power. The ruling dynasty of Copán saw Kawiil as their patron god.

Litter A seat on which a person may be carried by two or more people.

Macaw A type of parrot found in Central America.

Maya A people of Central America. From about AD 100 the Maya developed a complex civilization based on the intensive farming of tropical rain forest and marshy areas. They built great ceremonial cities of stone. Around the year 900 the civilization collapsed; we still don't know why.

Obsidian A type of very hard, glassy rock that can be split easily to create sharp edges.

Pleiades A constellation of stars.

Quiriguá A less important Mayan city close to Copán.

Shaman A holy man or priest who believes he can talk to the gods and visit the world of spirits by entering a trance.

Slingshot Small, rounded stones hurled from a sling.

Soothsayer A holy man or priest who believes he can divine the wishes and intentions of the gods.

Stele An upright stone slab or pillar carved with pictures and writing.

Tun The extended or long-count Mayan calendar. This dates the entire history of creation, starting in 3114 BC and ending in the year we call 2012.

Tzolk'in Haab The basic Mayan calendar, based on three interlinking cycles of 13, 20, and 365 days. It repeated itself every 52 years.

Wayeb The five days that occurred every 360 days and that did not fit into one of the 13 months of the Tzolk'in Haab. They were considered to mark the new year, and were sacred to the Maya.

Xibalba A land believed to lie beneath the ground, which takes the form of a series of stone palaces inhabited by powerful supernatural lords who are hostile to humans.

Index